Big Book of Words

Bob's Kitchen

hillside

shelter

Travis

Farmer Pickles

wheelbarrow

basket

Wendy

flower pots

Wendy loves growing things. Today, Muck and Scruffty have come to help her dig a vegetable patch so she can grow carrots, leeks and potatoes next to her cabbages. She can't wait for them to grow, so she can cook tasty dinners for her friends!

Farmer Pickles and Travis are taking JJ and some visitors on a tour around Sunflower Valley. Scruffty barks 'hello' as they go past Wendy's caravan.

Counting with Bob!

There is only 1 Bob!
Point to him and say the number 1.

Can you see 2 blue hard hats
on Wendy and Mr Bentley?
Point to each one as you count to 2.

Can you see 3 talkie-talkie units?
Point to each one as you count to 3.

Muck has found 4 squirrels.
Point to each one as you count to 4.

5

Scrambler races past 5 sunflowers.
Point to each one as you count to 5.

6

Can you see 6 mountains?
Point to each one as you count to 6.

7

Bob has 7 books.
Point to each one as you count to 7.

8

Scruffty finds 8 daisies.
Point to each one as you count to 8.

9

Here are 9 friends together.
Point to each one as you count to 9.

10

There are 10 flowers on the tree!
Point to each one as you count to 10.

At the Market

chickens

bakery stall

perch

Mr Sabatini

pies

goat

cakes

bread
rolls

bread

biscuits

baguettes

Bob

pen

palm tree

pear

melon

bananas

pineapple

chicks

grapes

Farmer
Pickles

hay bales

sheep

Mr Beasley

Cassia

Carlo

ducklings

ducks

Bob's Workshop

Dizzy

door

ladder

fire extinguisher

Wendy

bucket

saw

work bench

bricks

toolbox

sawdust

wood

paint pot

paint brush

set square

hacksaw

pliers

drill

hard hat

poster

clipboard

hammer

mallet

spanner

lathe

chisel

Pilchard

cupboard

trowel

Bob

torch

screwdriver

screws

pencil

notebook

ruler

nails

counter top

tape measure

Can you find . . .

a cake?

bread loaves?

a toy train?

some teddy bears?

buns

shelves

bread loaves

mop

jam tarts

cake

Mrs Bentley

cheese

pizza

jam

yoghurt

chicken

sausages

eggs

pork pies

wool

wellington
boots

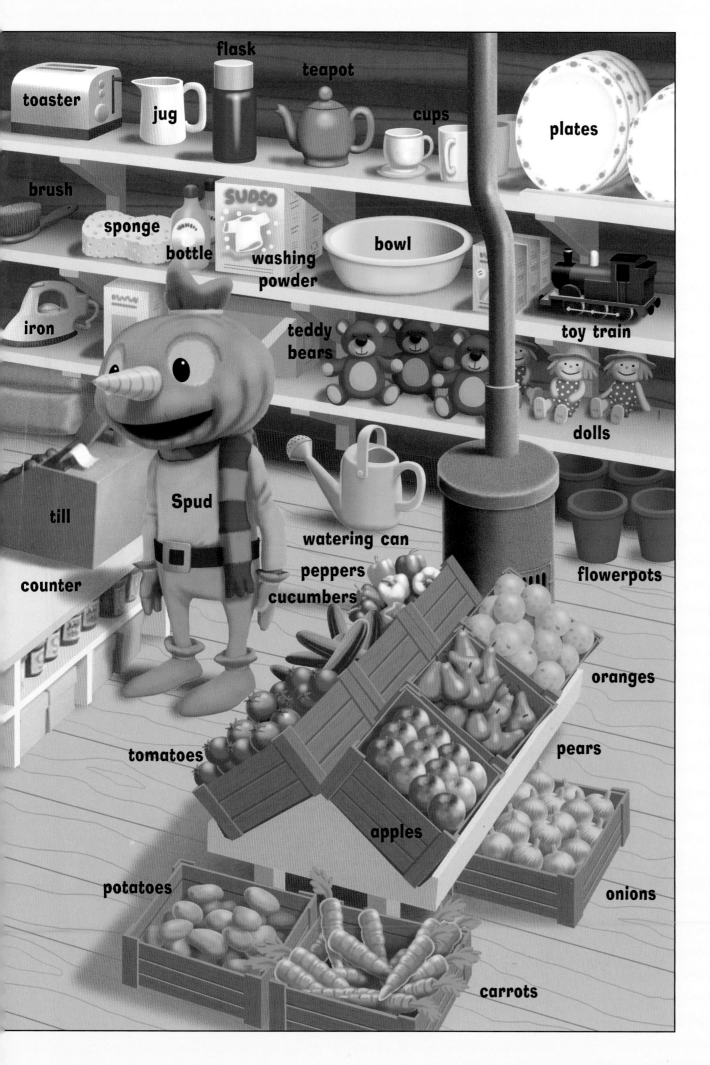

toaster
flask
teapot
jug
cups
plates
brush
sponge
bottle
washing powder
bowl
iron
teddy bears
toy train
Spud
dolls
till
watering can
flowerpots
counter
peppers
cucumbers
oranges
tomatoes
pears
apples
potatoes
onions
carrots

a teapot?

some plates?

a brush?

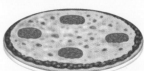

a pizza?

wellington boots?

At the Beach

At the Playground

crow

Spud

Pilchard

toy plane

rope bridge

skipping rope

Saffron

basketball

ramp

cricket bat

badminton racket
and shuttlecock

cricket ball

In the Countryside

owl

Bob

Scruffty

Scrambler

Path

Muck

badger

Pilchard

Wendy

sandwich

picnic rug

picnic basket

bowl

mouse

cake

crumbs

plate

can

knife
and fork

daisies

Spud's Bedroom

toy mouse

poster

lamp

picture frame

hammock bed

Spud

mug

chest of drawers

teddy bear

handkerchief

cake

book

marbles

blanket

socks

scarf

rug

skateboard

Sunflower Valley Shapes!

Can you find . . .

a diamond?

a star?

a triangle?

roof

flask

biscuits

mug

Roley

crate

cloud

tree

trowel

Bob

Wendy

wall

a circle?

a heart?

a square?

a rectangle?

At the Pond

Can you find . . .

a dragonfly?

bullrushes?

this duck?

brambles

bushes

frog

otter

Benny

Mr Beasley

fishing rod

Pilchard

oar · rowing boat

float

fish

pond

trees

dragonfly

rope

Bob

Wendy

bread

ducks

lilypads

bullrushes

lizard

an otter?

a lizard?

this fish?

a frog?

Colourful Sunflower Valley!

Scoop is yellow.

What other yellow things do you know?

Benny is pink.

What other pink things do you know?

Bob's coat is brown.

What other brown things do you know?

Roley is green.

What other green things do you know?

Lofty is blue.

What other blue things do you know?

Muck is red.

What other red things do you know?

Dizzy is orange.

What other orange things do you know?

Wendy's clothes are purple.

What other purple things do you know?

Let's Go Camping!

Birdie

shelter

flag

tent

Bob

flask

squirrels

Mrs Bentley   Mr Bentley

Wendy

water trough

otters

toolbox

leaves

bird table

Birdie's chicks

ropes

ladder

bird food

Dizzy

Mr and Mrs Bentley are camping in Sunflower Valley! They love waking up in their tent and seeing the countryside around them.

Bob and his team have built a special bird table nearby. Birdie and her chicks and lots of squirrels and otters are enjoying playing on it.

Today, Bob is topping up the water trough. He's really pleased to see the birds and animals having so much fun.

Autumn

Days of the Week

Monday

On Monday, Farmer Pickles asks Bob to build a storage shelter for him. It has to be ready for the grand opening of his factory on Sunday.

Tuesday

Early on Tuesday morning, Bob and the team get to work on building the bottle depot to store Farmer Pickles' bottles of sunflower oil.

Wednesday

On Wednesday, Sumsy comes to the factory. She gets to work with Scoop, lifting and stacking the boxes for delivery to the depot.

Thursday

On Thursday, disaster strikes! Some boxes of oil are knocked over and the bottles break. It takes a long time to clean up the mess.

Friday

By Friday, Bob has finished building the bottle depot. Farmer Pickles asks Sumsy and Scoop to deliver all the boxes of oil to the depot.

Saturday

On Saturday, Sumsy and Scoop are busy, travelling backwards and forwards, carrying boxes of oil. Soon they've finished the job.

Sunday

On Sunday, it's the Grand Opening Day. Farmer Pickles thanks the team for their help, as he declares the Sunflower Factory open!

At the Café

bats

moon

Bird

Roley

Mrs Sabatini

Spud

cake

pancakes

Farmer Pickles

Scruffty

Tell the Time with Bob

At 7 o'clock, Bob meets Wendy.
They are building the Dome today!

At 8 o'clock, Lofty, Scoop, Roley,
Muck and Dizzy arrive to help them.

By 9 o'clock, the foundations are laid.
Then Dizzy pours in the concrete.

At 10 o'clock, the Dome's wooden panels
and triangular windows arrive.

By 11 o'clock, Lofty has helped put the first section of windows on the Dome.

At 12 o'clock, Wendy has lunch with Mr and Mrs Bentley. They've invited everyone to the Dome opening party that night.

At 1 o'clock, Wendy asks Scrambler to take Scruffty for a run in the valley.

By 2 o'clock, they're racing through muddy puddles – splash!

Tell the Time with Bob

At 3 o'clock, Wendy asks Mr Bentley to fetch balloons for the opening party.

At 4 o'clock, Wendy calls Roley to flatten the ground before the party.

At 5 o'clock, Roley uses his talkie-talkie to call the other machines to the party.

By 6 o'clock, Wendy wonders if the Dome will be finished in time. Bob promises to get the job done!

At 7 o'clock, the Dome is ready!
Bob celebrates with his friends, before happily going home to bed.